basic business budgeting tips

Tammy Elliot
President & CEO of Perfect Wedding Guide

contents

praise for Tammy Elliot

"Tammy is the like the Suze Orman of the wedding industry. She is an informative speaker who gets you feeling like you want to take action now. I took away a lot of from her sessions and began implementing them as soon as I go home. Love her!"

"I've learned how to market and evaluate my marketing and financial goals. Her seminar was very informative and teaches me how to keep up with today's business."

"I enjoyed her presentation and felt that she had a lot of good information to share."

"Tammy's energy, vitality and ideas really got me excited to come back and go to work!"

"I really liked how she used layman's terms; everything was easily understandable and it was easy to relate and foresee areas where I could improve my business."

"Tammy was great. I loved her no BS approach. She provided lots of useful information; information that I will use to better my business."

introduction

If your goal is to be a "for profit" business and not a "non-profit" business, a budget is a must-have tool for planning, managing and achieving your financial success.

Too many small businesses believe their operation is too small for a formal budgeting process, or that the budgeting process is too complicated. They instead manage their business's finances from their checkbook based on the daily balance.

I'm here to tell you that no business is too small to go through the process of preparing a budget, and that it is vital to the daily management of their business.

why have a budget?

In a nutshell, you should create a budget so you know just how much money your business is taking in, how much money you need to spend to operate your business, and how much money you need to bring in in order to meet your goals.

Other reasons to create a budget include:

- It provides a road map
- Fosters good decision making throughout the year
- Helps manage surprises in your business and
- Offers understanding of where you stand financially with your business at all times

Another major benefit to having a budget is that it helps you minimize risks and plan for major expenditures. It's better to know if you can afford something – like a new lease or equipment - before your sign on the dotted line, rather than after, only to discover you can't afford the commitment.

You should build a budget annually, broken down by month. This will allow you to manage your finances throughout the year and give you better historical information to work with in the future.

bottom line

Every business needs a budget. Running a business without one is like taking a road trip without a map - you may have a destination in mind, but have no idea how to get where you're going.

2 How to create a budget

If you have budgets from previous years, the first thing you want to do is review them. How did you do against the budgets you created?

If you are building a budget for the first time, even though you have been in business, review bank statements, tax returns and sales contracts and expenses the best you can.

If you are building a budget for a new business, look at market research, examine similar businesses and research through local business groups.

Regardless of which scenario fits your circumstances, keep your budget simple. It doesn't have to be complicated. In fact, the simpler it is, the better.

Every budget needs the following components:

Basic Business Budgeting Tips

1. **Revenues**. Account for all revenue streams. If you provide more than one product or service, create separate revenue lines for each. This will allow you to see where your revenues are coming from, what is selling and track your expenses and profit from each.

2. **Costs/expenses.** Group your expenses together into categories if need be. Just make sure you understand what is included in each category. For example, it's not necessary to have a line item for each office expense, such as paper clips, phones or office space. Group these expenses into one category; Office Expense. Also, don't forget expenses like insurance, taxes and licenses.

3. **Profits/losses.** You will want to see what is left over once you calculate your income with your expenses. Are you making a profit or are you losing money?

bottom line

Keep your budget simple.

3 revenue

When forecasting revenue, you may want to use a conservative and aggressive approach. Like most small business owners, you will most likely fluctuate between a conservative reality and a dream state, which keeps you inspired.

Some things to consider when assessing revenue:

- Where is your revenue coming from?
- Do you have more than one revenue stream? For example, do you offer DJ services and up lighting? Do you provide photography and photo booths, flip books and videography?

Basic Business Budgeting Tips

- Be sure to identify all products and services you provide and calculate the income from each. I recommend you have separate revenue lines for each income stream. This will allow you to track your sales in each category and see if you are maximizing your potential or see which product/services are selling the best for you.
- How much revenue do you already have locked in for the year you are budgeting? How secure is it? What is your cancellation rate and policy? Are you at 25%, 30%, 50% of your revenue goal? In previous years, have you noticed any trends to how much revenue you've added in the year vs. going into the year with X on the books?
- Forecast the number of jobs you can execute (your availability) with your current structure. How does this compare to last year? Is your number aggressive or conservative?

When projecting revenue or preparing a sales forecast, be realistic yet challenging, and if need be err on the conservative side. Will revenues really double next year? Better to under-project, than over-project.

Do market research. What is happening with your product or service in your area? One of the biggest reasons for small business failure is the lack of market research.

13

Basic Business Budgeting Tips

Tips to create a Sales Forecast:

- **Create a target for your sales revenue** and/or look at revenue from last year and project it to increase, remain flat or decrease in revenue, based on your market and your business climate.
- **Figure what your average sale is worth.** (Total revenue/total # of sales = average sale)
- **Project your weddings/sales by month.** How do you expect to do each month? How does it compare to last year? If you are a new business, what is your goal? Remember, be realistic and yet challenging with your projection.
- **Pricing.** Are you underpricing or overpricing? Will this impact your average sale value?
    - ➢ Most common pricing mistakes: pricing based only on the cost to produce product/service, or basing your pricing on competitors' prices.
    - ➢ Tips for pricing: Cover cost of goods/services, cover marketing and overhead, factor in sales commissions and be competitive.

Basic Business Budgeting Tips

Market Research. Ask your associations for any information or research they have on the previous year and the upcoming year. Do they have any projections to share with you? Ask others in the industry and check with industry associations to see what they are hearing or projecting based on feedback from their members. What are they projecting – up, down or flat? Go to TheWeddingReport.com and pull some reports for your geographic area and for your industry. For a small fee you can gain access to important industry and market information that will help you know how much revenue is available in your area, levels of spending, number of weddings, and average spends for your product/service. Industry networking events are also a great place to find out the market buzz – just remember to check hearsay with facts.

Review market changes. Are there any factors impacting your region that are exclusive to your area? Are people/jobs moving in or out of your area or is it flat? Are any major industries moving in or out of the area that will impact population? You will also want to review the competitive landscape. Have there been any major changes in your area in your market? Have a number of new businesses cropped up in your space? Any national businesses moving into your area that will impact your business? How many have gone out of business and why? Are there any market trends popping up or fading out?

Review changes or planned changes to your business. Are you adding or eliminating any new products or services that generate revenue? Are you doing anything to increase revenue – marketing, adding another salesperson, or buying the assets of a competitor? Are you merging with anyone? Has any product or service you offer fallen out of favor or become the latest new trend in the wedding industry? If you are on the upside of a new trend, you have an opportunity; if you are on the downside of the trend, be prepared and have a plan.

SWOT analysis. Strengths, Weaknesses, Opportunities and Threats. Outline each of these areas for your business. When you recognize your strengths and weaknesses in the marketplace, you have a better opportunity to compete. When you can identify opportunities and threats within your marketplace, you are more likely to manage them. Search the web for free SWOT analysis information and instructions.

bottom line

One of the biggest reasons businesses fail is a lack of market research.

4 costs and expenses

It's important to identify and calculate every expense you have for your business, so there are no hidden costs or unexpected expenditures.

Break your expenses down into fixed costs and variable costs. **Fixed costs** are monthly predictable costs that do not change. **Variable costs** are the expenses that fluctuate from month to month.

Example of **fixed costs:**

- Rent
- Utility bills
- Phone/communications/internet costs
- Accounting/bookkeeping
- Legal/insurance/licensing fees
- Postage
- Technology
- Advertising & Marketing
- Salaries

Example of **variable costs:**

- Costs of goods sold
    - Materials & supplies
    - Packaging
- Direct labor costs
    - Customer service
    - Direct sales
    - Direct marketing

19

Basic Business Budgeting Tips

Tips you should follow when forecasting expenses:

- Double your estimates for advertising and marketing costs, since they are always more than projected
- Triple your estimates for legal, insurance and licensing fees, since they are very hard to predict and almost always exceed expectations.
- Keep track of direct sales & customer service time

Other expenses to be aware of when itemizing:

Annual goal expenses. Goal-related projects that should be factored into the budget. If you are projecting an increase of 15 percent in sales, the costs associated with the increase should be factored into the budget (commissions, marketing, supplies, etc.)

Contingency expenses. Expenses that handle unexpected costs. Don't forget to include repair/re-purchasing essential equipment when listing expenses.

Project Expenses. If you know you are undertaking a special project for your business that is a one-time expense, be sure to factor it into your budget. I usually have a long list of project expenses and add them to the budget by priority and available funds.

5 cutting/controlling expenses

As you prepare your budget, be sure to question every expense. As a small business owner, you can't afford to waste money.

For example, if you're paying $600 a month for web hosting, maybe it's time to get quotes and look for something cheaper. I make it a rule to get at least three quotes from different suppliers for comparison shopping. It's amazing how much you can save by doing this.

Sometimes we stick with the same supplier year after year, for things like phone service, insurance or copiers, because it's easier to just roll over your contracts from year to year.

By taking some time to look around and get quotes, you can save a lot of money. And remember, just because you bought it last year, doesn't mean you need it this year.

6 profit margins

Every organization should have a target profit margin. Profit margins allow for returns for business owners or investors, and allow you to reinvest into your business. Profits are important for all organizations and healthy profit margins are a strong indicator of the strength of a business.

What is the average profit margin for your business for each revenue stream? How do you compare?

bottom line

What is your target profit margin?

7 revisions

A budget revision process is not a one-time activity. In a well-managed operation, budgets are regularly revised, either in part or in whole, with the goal of increasing profits without decreasing the quality of your products or services.

Be sure you start the budgeting process well in advance, so you have plenty of time to evaluate your numbers and make changes before you lock it in for the year.

bottom line

Expect to take detours from your original budget. Things come up that you didn't expect, so make adjustments as needed.

8 cash flow management

You've heard it before: cash is king. This is especially true when it comes to the financial management of your company. The lag time between when you have to pay your suppliers and employees and the time you collect from your customers is the problem, and the solution is cash flow management.

Important components to cash flow management:

Accounts Receivable. A/R represents sales that have not yet been collected in the form of cash. An accounts receivable is created when you sell something to a customer in return for their promise to pay at a later date. To properly manage your cash flow, you must know the negative effects caused by the time it takes your customers to pay on their accounts.

Basic Business Budgeting Tips

Credit terms. These are the time limits you set for your customers' promise to pay for the product/service purchased from your business. Credit terms affect the timing of your cash inflows. Offering discounts is one way to improve early payment and cash flow.

Inventory. This describes the extra merchandise or supplies your business keeps on hand to meet the demands of customers. An excessive amount of inventory hurts your cash flow by using up money that could be used for other cash outflows.

Accounts payable and cash flow. These are amounts you owe to your suppliers that are payable sometime within the near future, meaning 30-90 days. Without payables and trade credit, you'd have to pay for all goods and services at the time you purchase them. For optimum cash flow management, you'll need to examine your payables schedules.

Prepare cash flow projections for next year, next quarter, and if you're on shaky ground, next week. An accurate cash flow projection can alert you to trouble well before it strikes.

Start your cash flow projection by adding cash on hand at the beginning of the period with other cash to be received from various sources. In the process, you will wind up gathering information from salespeople, service reps, collections, credit workers and your accounting department (which may be you). In all cases, you'll be asking the same question: How much cash – in the form of customer payments, interest earnings, service fees, partial collections of bad debts, down payments and the like – are we going to get in, and when?

The second part of making accurate cash flow projections is detailed knowledge of amounts and dates of upcoming cash outlays. That means not only knowing when each penny will be spent, but on what. Have a line item on your projection for every significant outlay, including rent, inventory (when purchased for cash), professional fees, utilities, office supplies, debt payments, advertising, vehicle and equipment maintenance and fuel.

As difficult as it is for a business owner to prepare projections, it's one of the most important things one can do. Projections rank in importance next to business plans and mission statements.

Basic Business Budgeting Tips

Ways to improve cash flow

1. **Improve receivables** by improving the speed at which you turn materials and supplies into products, inventory into receivables and receivables into cash

   - Offer discounts to customers who pay their bills rapidly.
   - Get rid of old, outdated inventory for whatever you can.
   - Issue invoices promptly and follow up immediately if payments are slow.
   - C.O.D. – Cash on Delivery.

2. **Managing Payables.** Anytime you see expenses growing faster than sales, examine costs carefully to find places to cut or control them. Here are some tips:

   - Take full advantage of creditor payment terms. If a payment is due in 30 days, don't pay it in 15.
   - Use electronic funds transfer to make payments on the last day they are due. You will remain current with suppliers while retaining use of your funds as long as possible.

- Communicate with suppliers so they know your financial situation. If you ever need to delay a payment you'll need their trust and understanding.
- Carefully consider vendors' offers of discounts for earlier payments. These can amount to expensive loans to your suppliers.
- Don't always focus on the lowest price when choosing suppliers. Sometimes more flexible payment terms can improve your cash flow more than a bargain-basement price.

Surviving Shortfalls

Sooner or later, you may find yourself running short on cash and unable to pay your bills. This doesn't mean you're a failure as a business person – you're a normal entrepreneur who can't perfectly predict the future.

The key to managing cash shortfalls is to become aware of the problem as early and accurately as possible. If you assume from the beginning that you will someday be short on cash, you can arrange for a line of credit at your bank. This allows you to borrow money up to a preset limit any time you need it. Since it's far easier to borrow when you don't need it, arranging a credit line before you are short is vital.

Basic Business Budgeting Tips

If you can't get cash or credit from a traditional bank, turn to your suppliers. You can often get extended terms that amount to a hefty, low-cost loan just by asking. That's especially true if you've been a good customer in the past and communicate about your financial situation.

Other areas to help when in a cash-flow crunch include finding a financial service to buy your receivables, speeding up payments from customers, selling unused office equipment and choosing the bills you pay very carefully. Don't just pay the smallest ones and let the rest sit. Make payroll first, crucial suppliers next and ask the rest if you can skip a payment or make a partial payment.

Best Tip: Build an emergency fund so you always have cash on hand.

bottom line

Cash is king, so be sure to manage it wisely.

9 ongoing evaluation

Your budget will do you no good if you leave it tucked in a drawer. In order to get the most benefit, be sure to view your actual revenue and expense numbers against your projected numbers. Are you on target? Do you need to re-calculate? Budgets are regularly revised, either in part or whole, so don't feel bad if you need to tweak your budgets from time to time.

Regular reviews will give you a closer relationship to your budget and business cycles. The more you know about the money coming in and going out, the better you will be able to make decisions for your business, spot trends and make necessary changes before it's too late.

10 free budgeting resources

Today you can go online to find just about anything you need to create a budget for your business, create forms, sales plans or business plans. Here a few sites to get you started:

sba.gov/category/type-form/small-business-forms

smallbusinessfreeforms.com/business_budget.html

formville.com/F876_Business-Budget.html

brighthub.com/office/entrepreneurs/topics/business-management.aspx

vertex42.com/ExcelTemplates/budgets.html

samplewords.com/cat/personal-business

Tammy Elliot joined Perfect Wedding Guide in 2004 as President and became CEO in 2010. She is responsible for all areas of operation and development for both PWG Franchising, LLC and PWG Publishing, LLC. Operating nationwide, PWG is a multi-platform media company for the wedding business that produces local publications, a planning website, database marketing, bridal shows and networking events.

With over 30 years of experience in marketing, sales, management and business, her career spans a multitude of mediums, where she managed, owned or consulted for numerous companies including radio, TV, cable, internet and print. She worked for or consulted many companies through many phases including, major growth, startups and turnarounds such as Disney/ABC Radio Group – Atlanta, Cox Communications, GAF Broadcasting, and Reams Broadcasting.

Tammy is a highly-rated speaker domestically and internationally . She is known for her no-nonsense approach to business and has presented at Wedding MBA, NACE, CaterSource, The Business of Weddings In Ireland, Weddings Beautiful in Cancun, IFA and many more.

perfectweddingguide.com

Made in the USA
Monee, IL
05 November 2026

67386155R00021